D1131687

SUPER
SANDCASTLE™
Animal Habitats

# What Lives in the Arctic?

**Oona Gaarder-Juntti**

Consulting Editor, Diane Craig, M.A./Reading Specialist

**ABDO**
Publishing Company

Published by ABDO Publishing Company, 8000 West 78th Street, Edina, Minnesota 55439. Copyright © 2009 by Abdo Consulting Group, Inc. International copyrights reserved in all countries. No part of this book may be reproduced in any form without written permission from the publisher. Super SandCastle™ is a trademark and logo of ABDO Publishing Company.

Printed in the United States.

Credits
Editor: Liz Salzmann
Content Developer: Nancy Tuminelly
Cover and Interior Design and Production: Oona Gaarder-Juntti, Mighty Media
Illustration: Oona Gaarder-Juntti
Photo Credits: AbleStock, Creatas, Digital Vision, iStockphoto/John Fugett, ShutterStock

**Library of Congress Cataloging-in-Publication Data**

Gaarder-Juntti, Oona, 1979-

  What lives in the Arctic? / Oona Gaarder-Juntti.

     p. cm. -- (Animal habitats)

  ISBN 978-1-60453-172-5

  1.  Zoology--Arctic regions--Juvenile literature. 2.  Animals--Arctic regions--Juvenile literature.. I. Title.

  QL105.G33 2008

  591.70911'3--dc22

                    2008005475

Super SandCastle™ books are created by a team of professional educators, reading specialists, and content developers around five essential components— phonemic awareness, phonics, vocabulary, text comprehension, and fluency— to assist young readers as they develop reading skills and strategies and increase their general knowledge. All books are written, reviewed, and leveled for guided reading, early reading intervention, and Accelerated Reader® programs for use in shared, guided, and independent reading and writing activities to support a balanced approach to literacy instruction.

# About SUPER SANDCASTLE™

## Bigger Books for Emerging Readers
## Grades K–4

Created for library, classroom, and at-home use, Super SandCastle™ books support and engage young readers as they develop and build literacy skills and will increase their general knowledge about the world around them. Super SandCastle™ books are part of SandCastle™, the leading PreK–3 imprint for emerging and beginning readers. Super SandCastle™ features a larger trim size for more reading fun.

### Let Us Know
Super SandCastle™ would like to hear your stories about reading this book. What was your favorite page? Was there something hard that you needed help with? Share the ups and downs of learning to read. We want to hear from you! Send us an e-mail.

**sandcastle@abdopublishing.com**

Contact us for a complete list of SandCastle™, Super SandCastle™, and other nonfiction and fiction titles from ABDO Publishing Company.

www.abdopublishing.com • 8000 West 78th Street Edina, MN 55439 • 800-800-1312 • 952-831-1632 fax

The Arctic is the part of the earth that is farthest north. It includes the Arctic Ocean and the frozen land around it. The center of the Arctic Ocean is covered with ice.

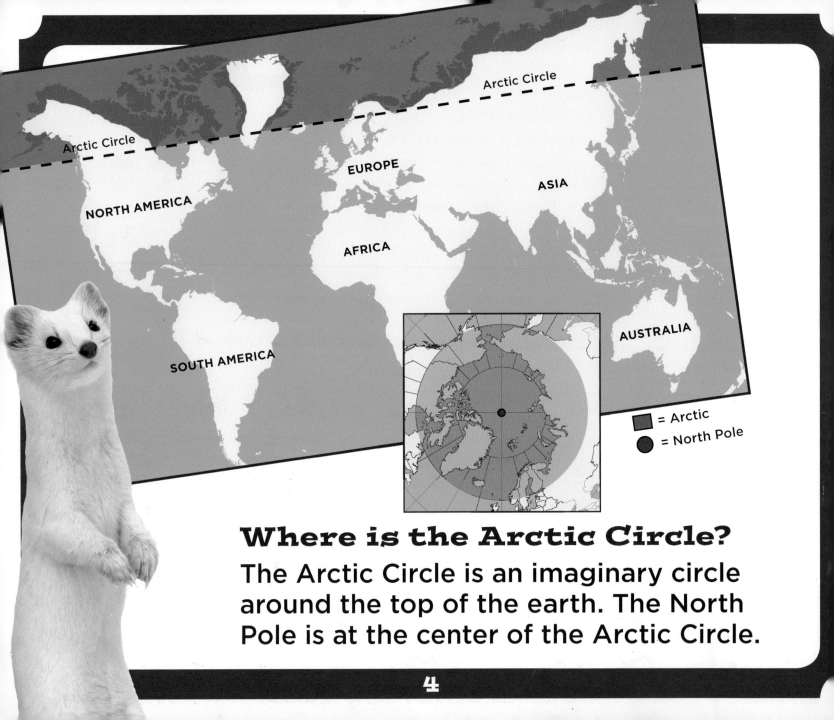

Arctic Circle

Arctic Circle

EUROPE

ASIA

NORTH AMERICA

AFRICA

SOUTH AMERICA

AUSTRALIA

■ = Arctic
● = North Pole

# Where is the Arctic Circle?

The Arctic Circle is an imaginary circle around the top of the earth. The North Pole is at the center of the Arctic Circle.

# What does the Arctic look like?

The land in the Arctic is called the arctic tundra. It is frozen and treeless. Few plants, such as grass and lichen, grow in the Arctic.

# ATLANTIC PUFFIN

**Animal class: Bird**
**Location: Arctic**

Atlantic puffins spend most of their time at sea. Puffins make nests on rocky cliffs in the spring. Females lay a single egg. The male and female puffins take turns caring for the egg.

Puffins dive under water to catch herring and other small fish to eat.

# ARCTIC FOX

**Animal class: Mammal**
**Location: Arctic**

Arctic foxes walk on top of the snow. They listen for small animals that are underneath. Arctic foxes have the warmest fur of any mammal.

Arctic foxes have white fur in the winter and gray or brown fur in the summer.

# SNOWY OWL

**Animal class: Bird**
**Location: Arctic**

Snowy owls have excellent hearing and eyesight. Snowy owls can find their prey even if it's hidden under the snow. Unlike other owls, snowy owls hunt during the day.

Snowy owls have white feathers to help them blend in with their surroundings. Females have more brown spots than males.

10

# HARP SEAL

**Animal class: Mammal**
**Location: Arctic**

Harp seals are all white when they are born. This makes it harder for predators to see baby seals on the ice. Their coats turn darker and develop spots when they're older.

Harp seals spend most of their adult lives in the ocean. They can stay underwater for up to 15 minutes.

# WALRUS

**Animal class: Mammal**
**Location: Arctic**

Walruses have tusks that can grow up to three feet long. Walruses use their tusks to help pull themselves out of the water. They eat sea creatures like shrimp, clams, and crabs.

Walruses are very social and live in herds. A herd can have more than 100 walruses.

14

# BELUGA WHALE

**Animal class: Mammal**
**Location: Arctic**

Beluga whales travel in groups called pods. Belugas are very vocal and communicate with clicks and whistles.

Unlike most other whales, the beluga whale has a flexible neck. It can turn its head in all directions.

# Musk Ox

**Animal class: Mammal**
**Location: Arctic**

Musk oxen roam the Arctic looking for food. They eat grass, lichen, and willows. They have a thick, shaggy overcoat and a softer undercoat to keep them warm.

Musk oxen stand in a circle around their calves to protect them.

# POLAR BEAR

**Animal class: Mammal**
**Location: Arctic**

Polar bears are good swimmers and can see well underwater. They have an excellent sense of smell. A polar bear can smell a seal beneath the ice a mile away.

A polar bear's large feet are like snow shoes. They are also furry to keep the polar bear from sliding on the ice.

# Have you ever been to the Arctic?

# More Arctic Animals

Can you learn about these Arctic animals?

arctic hare
arctic tern
caribou
collared lemming
Dall sheep

ermine
gyrfalcon
moose
narwhal
reindeer
rock ptarmigan
ruddy turnstone
snow bunting
snow goose
wolverine

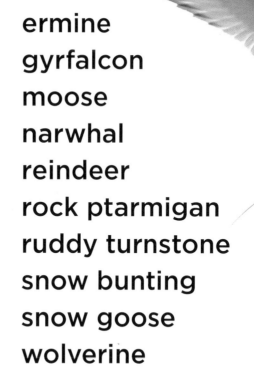

# GLOSSARY

**blend** – to match or mix things together so that you can't tell one from the other.

**develop** – to grow or change over time.

**female** – being of the sex that can produce eggs or give birth. Mothers are female.

**flexible** – easy to move or bend.

**lichen** – a kind of plant that grows on a hard surface such as a rock or tree.

**male** – being of the sex that can father offspring. Fathers are male.

**mammal** – a warm-blooded animal that has hair and whose females produce milk to feed the young.

**predator** – an animal that hunts others.

**protect** – to guard someone or something from harm or danger.

**tusk** – a long, sharp tooth that sticks out of an animal's mouth.

**vocal** – able to use the voice to make sounds or communicate.